RIDING the WAVES

A Guide for the Manager in State Government

Dianne G. Davis

CONTENTS

INTRODUCTION

The life of a manager in state government is as predictable as the weather at sea. The waves of the sea cannot be controlled and can change without warning. A meteorologist can provide a forecast of probable weather conditions; however, Mother Nature has the last laugh. Weather conditions can cause a wide array of emotions from fear and anxiety to calm and peacefulness.

A manager is subject to rapidly changing conditions on any given day. She may be subjected to harmful conditions because of ineffective leadership, an angry public, an unsatisfied customer, or a powerful political force. She may be equally impacted by positive conditions because of effective leadership, a content public, a satisfied customer, or a powerful political force.

I was a regional director or middle manager for a government program for 15 years. I was intrigued with the variety of managerial and leadership traits that I observed in my tenure with the agency. What makes a manager effective and efficient? What traits and characteristics inspire staff and create public trust? I began keeping a journal of effective and efficient traits and characteristics that inspire employees and create public trust. The vast majority of managers with whom I worked was effective and efficient and worked within the boundaries of policy and procedures.

Alternately, my journal contains the ineffective and inefficient traits and characteristics of managers and leaders that cause employees to exit the agency and create public distrust. Negative managerial traits do nothing to inspire subordinates and cause the public to respond negatively to the agency. It was my experience that it takes ten effective and efficient managers to undo the harm that is caused by one ineffective and inefficient manager. The consequences of ineffective and inefficient management will lead to unproductive and discouraged employees, inexcusable expenditure of funds, and a lack of focus on client services.

It's very easy to navigate the waters that are smooth, clear, and calm. It's very tedious and difficult to navigate through waters that are bumpy, dark, and chaotic. An individual cannot control the weather and a manager cannot control the actions of an elected official, changes in policy and procedures, and an abrupt change in management. She can; however, choose how she will react to various changes, both good and bad. State government needs managers and leaders who have courage, are ethical, and assume responsibility for their actions.

Riding the Waves is a compilation of effective and efficient managerial traits and ineffective and inefficient managerial traits and the contrasting effects of these managerial traits on subordinates and agency stakeholders. It's a quick read for managers and employees in state government. My Christian faith grew stronger in my final years of management because of my desire to find encouragement and strength. I read numerous books and other publications while I worked in state government in search of inspiration and coping skills. I never read a book on management or leadership that had more meaning than the books of Proverbs and James in the Bible (NIV).

TEMPEST TOSSED
MANAGEMENT IN STATE GOVERNMENT

What traits and characteristics make a manager in state government effective and efficient? What makes a manager a good custodian of a taxpayer's money? Management in state government is physically, emotionally, and intellectually demanding. A manager is sandwiched between his respective supervisor and his respective subordinates and is presumed to be a fountain of information. Information flows into this fountain and out of this fountain via e-mail, web mail, voicemail, and snail mail. A manager in this position is required to process information and present it to subordinates, his supervisor, and the public in a manner that is practical, diplomatic, and cordial.

A balanced manager must learn to ride the waves in public sector employment. He may be surrounded by an angry public, corrupt elected officials, state employees lacking work ethics and little ambition, state employees performing multiple tasks for low wages, and a demanding supervisor. The manager must learn to effectively navigate the waters in the midst of a strong tropical cyclone. In my first five years of management, I was subjected to a massive reorganization and a merger with another department. As such, my book is primarily focused on my days as a regional director or middle manager. My perception of this job is that of riding a raft in the middle of an ocean with constant threats of a storm that may sink the vessel. I was attracted to state government because of an attractive retirement package, annual leave, sick leave, and a flexible work environment. There are not as many incentives for working in the public sector today.

A person typically obtains employment at an entry-level position in state government because she thinks state government is a safe and secure haven for employment. The individual usually has an innate desire to work in a helping profession or in an organization that serves the public. An effective employee will quickly climb the state employment ladder if she has the skills, a good work ethic, and ambition. She will be promoted into management with no other road to take in a short period of time unless she guards her potential.

Managers try to remove barriers and provide leadership that is so desperately needed by their frontline employees. But managers in state government are not created equal. As I have already mentioned, there are effective managers, and there are ineffective managers. My supervisors or managers were located in Atlanta and my office was in Southwest Georgia, 200 miles away from the main office. Communication was a significant issue because of the distance between our offices. Some managers made themselves very available to my inquiries and concerns. With them, I felt I had partners at work. However, some managers hid in their corner offices in Atlanta and did not respond to inquiries or concerns. These managers may as well have been located in Siberia.

My inspiration for this book has been the managers I worked with – both good and bad. It is a survival kit for all managers and potential managers. I have worked with seventeen senior-level managers, twenty-four middle managers, and nine line managers with different characteristics, talents, traits, and ethical standards. These managers have had a lasting impact on my career and the career I will pursue following retirement from state government. Most managers are middle of the road. They are ordinary people who aspire to help their employees overcome barriers and perform work at an optimal level. Today, as a taxpayer, I remain concerned about managers and leaders in state government for entirely different reasons. I prefer that the taxpayers' money be spent effectively and efficiently.

There are managers who react to situations poorly. No plan of action is ever implemented. Their responses are an effort to divert attention from the real problems that exist in state government. Some managers react with nervousness and cowardice because of fear of negative consequences. There is no effort to resolve problems. The energy and effort are diverted toward covering problems and keeping the public uninformed. Unfortunately, some managers today do not plan for the future. They survive in the present and repeat mistakes either they or others have made in the past. They simply adjust their sails to whatever atmospheric conditions may exist from day to day.

In contrast, there are managers who demonstrate courage and seek solutions that are in the best interest of agency stakeholders. There are managers who plan for the future and are accountable for decisions that are made. It is refreshing and invigorating to work with a manager who acknowledges mistakes, seeks viable solutions, and is transparent. He is a friend to coworkers, taxpayers, legislators, and the public that the agency serves.

State employees who read this book can make conscientious decisions about managerial positions in state government. We need good managers in government. They are in short supply. Employment in state government has become entirely too unattractive to qualified applicants. An individual with a strong work ethic, a good education, and a positive attitude can write his ticket in the private sector. There are few incentives to attract the best minds to jobs in the public sector. A talented employee in the private sector can earn three times the pay as in state government.

A state employee will find himself or herself working for and with some of the employees described in this book. Unfortunately, the future of state employment does not look good. Individuals who choose to work in the public sector know they will never be rich. Their desire is to experience an intrinsically rewarding career and be able to comfortably pay for living expenses. Excellent employees with a work ethic are paid the same meager wages as incompetent employees who do not have a work ethic. State employees have shouldered the decreased state agency budgets through their salaries. When the economy takes a turn upward, state government will only be able to retain employees who cannot find employment in the private sector. State government is rapidly becoming the primary employer of mediocre workers. It is a sad state of affairs for the taxpayer.

There are numerous references to the Christian faith in my book. My faith has played a significant role in my career and has been very evident in many of the effective and efficient employees I have known. It is my perception that government leaders would make more decisions that are in the best interest of the public if more leaders took the time to consult with the Lord. Public sector employees and agency stakeholders deserve leadership that is effective and efficient. It is my opinion that people with disabilities have not always received the services they deserve because, for example, the government agencies dedicated to serving this population have not always had effective and efficient leadership.

THE STORM
THE INEFFECTIVE AND INEFFICIENT MANAGER

An effective and supportive manager can make up for difficult circumstances, inexplicable policies, cumbersome procedures, hostile environments, and low morale. An ineffective and unsupportive manager creates difficult circumstances, inexplicable policies, cumbersome procedures, and hostile environments. A storm is created in the working environment with any combination of negative leadership and managerial traits. Ineffective and inefficient managers are more abundant in state government because the manager in the public sector does not always have to produce positive results or measureable outcomes. The private sector requires a manager to produce a profit for the company or some other measureable outcome. This chapter addresses the various styles of ineffective and inefficient management. It is based on negative traits in leadership and management that may produce storms within an agency. I placed this chapter in the beginning of the book so the reader would have time to think about the negative consequences of poor leadership. The last chapter is dedicated to the effective and efficient characteristics in leadership and management.

I have a friend who is a teacher in an elementary school. She loves her job and her students, and they love her. I recall that she once had an ineffective manager, or, in her case, a principal. The principal provided nothing but negative feedback to teachers and appeared to have a predominantly negative attitude toward her subordinates. Because of this, my friend was eventually transformed from a teacher who loved her job into an employee who hated going to work. It happened in the course of a year. Her experience had a significant impact on me personally because I could observe the difference in her desire to perform optimally. The change was startling. I made a mental note to never focus on the negative characteristics of my coworkers.

This critical and judgmental manager did not motivate my friend or anyone else in the school. This type of management had the opposite effect. Teachers who had a high morale deteriorated, and the atmosphere and school environment, which had always been very pleasant, deteriorated quickly.

There were instances when I wanted to micromanage or perceive my employees in a negative light. These negative thoughts did not last long, however; because I recall what a critical and judgmental manager did to my friend and her colleagues.

There are two basic types of ineffective managers in state government. They are polar opposites, but both are destructive in nature. One type of manager is unresponsive and indecisive. This person is vague and provides very little guidance or leadership. She does not respond to phone calls, e-mails, or memos. She will not provide answers or guidance to critical concerns or issues. As a subordinate, you feel as though you are on a raft floating adrift in the sea. There is no wind to sail your vessel; you simply float. You hope for the best and pray that the worst does not happen.

The second type of ineffective manager is someone who practices micromanagement and needs to be in control at all times. He is the opposite of the unresponsive manager. He does not allow subordinates to make decisions. Ineffective and inefficient managers are promoted to positions of authority in state government because there are too few checks and balances for managers. An ineffective manager may go unnoticed by senior level management if there is no outcry from the public or from subordinates. An ineffective manager can blame others for poor management of limited resources. He or she can site policies as their reasons for unexplainable decisions. These types of managers can also suck up to their bosses and hide behind their coattails. Many ineffective and inefficient managers have ascended to heights because of relationships with their superiors or because they were adept at blaming coworkers for their mistakes.

Indecisiveness: An indecisive manager creates difficulties for employees because she does not provide answers or guidance to concerns her employees have in the field. This manager doesn't know the answer. Often, e-mails to them receive no response. Phone calls are not returned. It's as if the e-mail disappears into cyberspace or is written in some unintelligible language. There is no sense of urgency to respond to inquiries. When she does respond, her answers are usually vague and have no substance. This manager cannot answer questions without a consultation with human resources. Her favorite strategy is to wait and hope the question will go away. She does not have the necessary knowledge to be in a managerial position. She has not received training from the agency and has not acquired the skills to make appropriate decisions. She was probably promoted because of a relationship with a superior.

Indecisive managers typically do not have the self-confidence to make decisions. There is an excellent reason for the lack of self-confidence. The manager does not have the skills and knowledge to support subordinates or make decisions. The bigger problem with an indecisive manager is that she will surround herself with more indecisive subordinates because her greatest fear is that someone will find out she does not have the necessary skills and knowledge to perform the essential functions of her position.

Unresponsiveness: A manager who is unresponsive creates difficulties for subordinates because he cannot or will not answer questions. It is difficult to get in touch with the unresponsive manager. Voicemail and e-mail are ignored by the unresponsive manager. This type of management is born from a lack of passion for his work. The unresponsive manager usually has a secondary job that he values more than his government job, needs the health insurance, or is working toward an advanced college degree. This manager may not really be vested in his present job. He simply earns a paycheck with a few benefits and does not want to be bothered by employees or clients. This manager is content as long as he is not contacted by employees, customers, or the public.

This manager has usually not demonstrated any measurable skills or talents. He has advanced his career through his network of friends. He may have information that is valuable to a political liaison. Some unresponsive managers have considerable charm, which they use to advance their careers. There is little substance. Their speeches and presentations are not up-to-date. The words seldom change. This type of manager is dangerous because he does not have the desire to perform the essential functions of his position. He does not have the necessary work ethic.

This type of leadership style may be referred to as laissez-faire. The leader's role is peripheral, and employees manage their own areas of the agency. The leader evades the duties of management, causing uncoordinated delegation to occur. There is little communication from the top. Subordinates are left to fend for themselves. This type of leadership may produce a few creative superstars for the agency because of the lack of direction. A superstar will emerge to provide creative and productive solutions to problems in the agency. But more than likely, this leadership style produces dissatisfaction for employees.

There may be a more compelling reason for an employee's rapid ascent into management. It is worth paying attention to promotions when the person who is promoted has no real work accomplishments. An unresponsive manager may have engaged in an inappropriate physical relationship with his boss. An ineffective manager may also have a sweetheart deal with the boss. The boss may provide perks and opportunities that are not legally permitted through state government. For example, tax payers are not responsible for living accommodations, transportation to and from work, or personal media devices. Fortunately, the Office of the Inspector General (OIG) was founded to investigate improper use of funds to certain employees of the state. An employee can report the abuse of power to OIG in an anonymous manner and does not have to fear retaliation.

Dishonesty: A dishonest manager will use words to make points that are unfounded. Be concerned about your salary if you find yourself with a supervisor who tries to instill in your psyche that your work is your calling. This style of management is a strategy used to divert your attention from the fact that you do not get paid a salary commensurate with the responsibilities you have. This manager is not embarrassed to stand before a group and advise attendees that they do not work for money, only job satisfaction. An employee cannot experience job satisfaction if the pay is so low that she cannot meet her basic needs to provide a roof over her head, put food on the table, and pay medical expenses. This manager thinks people prefer recognition over money. A person can't concentrate on recognition and advancement when she's hungry, cold, and cannot pay for her medical insurance.

A dishonest manager will make verbal agreements or commitments that never come to pass. The dishonest manager will become proficient at putting a spin on everything. She may be referred to as a spin doctor. A spin doctor will twist a report or data to her advantage. She will also make the data appear favorable or beneficial to the agency. A dishonest manager will require staff to write white papers to support her position on self-serving projects. A verbal agreement should never be dismissed. How can anyone trust a manager who does not honor her verbal agreements? A dishonest manager creates an atmosphere of distrust and dissatisfaction.

Promises that cannot be honored are made by the dishonest manager. An example is a verbal promise for a salary increase made to an employee in exchange for the employee assuming additional responsibilities. The manager may not have the authority to approve the salary increase or may never intend to approve the salary increase. Either example will cause dissatisfaction and resentment among subordinates that are impacted by such verbal promises.

Closed mindedness: This manager does not accept other opinions or goals. He is headstrong and will not change his mind for any reason. He will research and find data to support his position on issues. A dedicated researcher can find data to support any position. It never occurs to this manager that there may be better solutions. This manager cannot accept that he may be wrong. Not only does he have a closed mind, but he has a closed door policy as well. He sits at his desk behind a closed door to prevent access by subordinates who do not support his decisions.

A closed-minded manager will harp on production as if government employees operate an assembly line making widgets. We work with people. The economic factors that plague our state and nation play no role in her efforts to increase production. Production at any cost is her number-one priority. For example, an agency may assist people with disabilities to employment, and there are few opportunities for employment. There are few opportunities for people without a disability, much less someone with a disability. The agency may not be able to fill vacant positions because of funding. This too will impact productivity. A closed minded manager will ignore all indicators that influence production and will continue to focus on the bottom line.

Employees may become ill because of the stress, and will begin to miss work. The closed minded manager does not think there is any legitimate reason to miss work, including illnesses. Employees throughout the state will have the same goals and expectations under the direction of a closed minded manager. It will not matter that there is a significant economic and cultural difference in South and North Georgia. This manager will make analogies to the private sector as though an employee in the public sector has the same level of authority and the same level of support and resources.

Hypocrisy: The hypocritical manager may hide behind her religious faith. She makes references to her religious views to demonstrate a false sense of transparency and compassion. She lives by her mantra of "do as I say, not as I do." The hypocritical manager requires employees to share travel while she drives solo or in her assigned state-owned vehicle. She advises employees to be content with a mediocre salary while she thinks of methods to increase her salary.

Verbal commitments should be taken seriously and should be honored. Be very wary of the manager who does not honor her verbal commitments. Prayer is the only advice I can give you if you find yourself supervised by a hypocrite. The hypocritical manager has no conscience. Her actions are similar to that of a sociopath. A sociopath is interested only in his personal needs and desires, without concern for the effects of her behavior on others.

Be wary and skeptical of the hypocritical manager who hides behind her religion. This manager forces subordinates to follow rules that she perceives are beneath her position. Watch the actions of the hypocrite. Actions speak louder than words. Actions will be the key to the individual's convictions and philosophy. This manager may communicate through words that indicate she is very religious. Do not trust the words. Do not take them at face value.

The next three negative characteristics are centered on the need to be in control of employees. The following ineffective characteristics are sometimes referred to as bully management.

Micromanagement: A micromanager must be in control of subordinates at all times. She has an autocratic style of management. She makes decisions unilaterally and closely supervises subordinates. Most micromanagers think they must be in constant control of employees and every aspect of the organization. This sense of control becomes unmanageable for the micromanager as she ascends the ladder. The larger the organization, the less chance the individual has of controlling all aspects of the organization.

Managers who have a need to control do not trust their subordinates. They believe subordinates do not take pride in their work and must be pushed and prodded daily. The micromanager has a need to be contacted by subordinates prior to any decision being made. It becomes profoundly difficult for the micromanager to maintain this level of control once she leaves the front line of management. A frontline supervisor may be able to micromanage her subordinates to some degree, but it becomes very difficult to be involved in all decisions once you enter middle management and beyond. It is wise for a micromanager to be content with frontline supervision. A frontline manager can have a certain level of control over her schedule and the day-to-day operations of her unit.

The micromanager is anal retentive. This terminology was coined by Sigmund Freud and still has application in our society today. The anal-retentive manager is obsessed with details and applies the same logic to the decision-making processes. One of the strategies of the anal-retentive personality is to keep subordinates unusually busy with paperwork, statistical research, reports, and other mindless activities. The anal-retentive manager must review all aspects of a project from start to finish. She must review agendas to determine the necessity of a meeting. She reads contracts prior to signing them although the contract writer has written countless similar documents in the past. She badgers employees about protocol that has been in existence for years.

A micromanager provides primarily negative feedback to her subordinates. She promotes an atmosphere that is counterproductive to effectiveness and efficiency. Micromanagers use words such as "mandatory meetings"; "this is a directive"; "this is incorrect"; "signatures are required"; and "must be observed." Her intentions are to motivate subordinates through negative remarks. However, her actions will have the opposite effect on staff.

A micromanager subscribes to the Theory X management style recognized by Douglas McGregor in *The Human Side of Enterprise* published in 1960. Theory X managers believe that workers are basically lazy and must be prodded like cattle to get any work completed. The Theory X characteristics will shine and the manager will write negative comments on performance appraisals. Micromanagers are unable to see the big picture. A micromanager will only see that an individual did not achieve her vision for the job responsibilities. The micromanager does not appear to be aware of extracurricular occurrences that may influence whether an individual achieved his goal.

A true micromanager thinks her way is the only way. Her attitude is "it's my way or the highway." Most employees will take the highway and leave the agency. It is my opinion, based on observation, that this trait will cause valuable professionals to exit a government agency in droves. Professional employees will compensate in a variety of ways for the other ineffective traits; however, they will run for cover when supervised by a micromanager.

Retaliation: A retaliatory manager will set the stage for failure. His expectations will not be realistic. The retaliatory manager manages the personnel budget as if it were his personal bank account. This penchant for saving tax dollars would be notable if he led by example and practiced the same principals. The retaliatory manager does not apply the same restrictions to his salary. His salary will continue to soar while subordinates must shoulder the brunt of inefficient funding. He will require staff to work in cubicles and poor environmental conditions. Some offices rented or owned by state government have ceilings that leak whenever it rains. Other offices are cohabited by rats, mice, and roaches. The mold in some offices causes allergic reactions and sinus infections. A retaliatory manager will require proof through medical documentation that the office environment is making employees sick. It's a no-brainer that poor environmental conditions can lead to allergic reactions and sinus infections. This manager may use corner offices in several different locations in the state while requiring staff to work in cubicles and cramped quarters. He will require coworkers to ride in compact rental cars or be reimbursed at the lowest travel rate while he drives a state owned car furnished by the taxpayers.

Vindictiveness: The vindictive manager will impose hardships on subordinates. Vindictive managers practice methods of torture in addition to methods of intimidation. A vindictive manager will search for opportunities to punish subordinates. Meetings are held in a location that is convenient for the manager and totally impractical for the employees and the taxpayer. Meetings will begin at eight in the morning and will end at six in the evening, ten hours of nonstop torture aimed at the derriere and head. Meetings will be located in uncomfortable settings such as the state office with uncomfortable chairs, an uncomfortable room temperature, and poor acoustics. There will be no funds for snacks or coffee and few opportunities for breaks.

The vindictive manager will make it impossible to schedule a vacation without negative consequences. Meetings will begin at eight on Monday morning so the employees must travel on Sunday afternoon. There is no consideration for personal lives. Employees may be required to travel to Atlanta for work-related functions on Mother's Day, Father's Day, Memorial Day, Labor Day, and Veteran's Day.

Vindictive managers may cause financial torture as well as physical torture. Managers who live outside the Atlanta perimeter are forced to stay in a hotel and eat meals in Atlanta. It costs a small fortune to attend monthly meetings in Atlanta. It's cheaper for taxpayers for meetings to convene in a central location; however, it's not as convenient for a boss who lives in Atlanta. An employee must pay for lodging, meals, and gas from his personal income. A travel statement for reimbursement of expenses is submitted following the trip. The reimbursement may take approximately five weeks. Hence, the cost may accumulate some interest on an employee's personal credit card.

Another tool used by a vindictive manager is the performance appraisal document. A performance appraisal can be used as a type of reward or a time to compliment and praise coworkers. The vindictive manager does not see it this way. The vindictive manager uses the performance appraisal as a document to intimidate and demoralize an individual. The vindictive manager will concentrate his efforts on finding the mistakes the individual committed over the course of a year. He will intentionally omit the positive accomplishments of the individual. He appears to take some pleasure in making a subordinate feel worthless and invaluable.

There may be a plausible and acceptable reason for an unproductive year. The employee may have been ill. A member of his family may have been ill. He may have had chemotherapy. There are no reasonable explanations to the vindictive manager. The vindictive manager thinks goals should be achieved at any expense, including health. The vindictive manager will assume the individual did not meet his goal because he is lazy and does not have organizational commitment.

One of the most decisive ways to anger or depress employees is to make them responsible for something they have no control over. It is a helpless and worthless feeling to be blamed for failure. The vindictive manager never seems to learn that this type of tyranny and management will backfire at a critical time. Humiliation and intimidation cause several severe reactions in employees. Your employees will get the last laugh eventually.

Any combination of these negative managerial traits will ignite a storm within the agency. Employees will look elsewhere and will leave the agency en mass. Seasoned employees will begin to count their days until retirement and will begin the transition to retirement long before necessary. Employees will seek ways to sabotage the agency and will focus on their misery rather than focus on the services to customers and the public. Employees of the agency, customers of the agency and the taxpayers suffer because of the manager. Employees will seek ways to sabotage the agency and will focus on their miserable state of being rather than on the public the agency is intended to serve. The following employee behaviors may indicate that a storm is brewing.

1. **Malaise:** The subordinate will stop working diligently and will become lethargic. He will slow down and move like a turtle. He will dread hearing the alarm clock in the morning. He will find excuses to be late for work. A normally energetic employee will become subdued and uninspired. It may become difficult for an employee to rouse himself from bed each morning. He will be drained by mid-afternoon and counting the moments until he is free for the day.

2. **Sabotage:** Employees will begin to fail. They will not assume ownership of the flow of work. Employees will deliberately quit making contributions to discussions. They will refuse to work overtime. No one will participate in extracurricular activities. Employees will embrace failure because they cannot see any positive benefits in working for success.

3. **Fear:** Fear can paralyze an employee. She may become afraid to take risks because of potential mistakes and may be content to stay in a box. She will not do anything to bring attention on herself. She will become afraid to move outside her comfort zone. Employees begin to fear any contact with the ineffective manager. Employees avoid phone calls, do not respond to e-mails, and run for cover when in the presence of the ineffective manager.

4. **Absenteeism:** Employees will find reasons not to report to work. They will call in sick or advise their coworkers

that a family member is sick. They will take unnecessary leave so they do not have to report to work. Employees in key positions can really wreak havoc in this frame of mind. A receptionist who doesn't show up to work causes multiple problems. A counselor who does not report to work when appointments are scheduled is a major headache for a manager. Work-related trips may have to be canceled if an employee bails out at the last minute.

5. **Poor morale:** No employee wants to be micromanaged. It is annoying and unnecessary especially when the person works in a professional setting. Poor morale causes long conversations at the water cooler. It causes staff to congregate in the break room or congregate in one office behind closed doors. Poor morale is contagious. It consumes the office like a wildfire. It drowns the spirit like a torrential rain.

An ineffective and inefficient manager can be identified. This manager is not honest and has no integrity. Ethical principles may as well be written in a foreign language. The manager creates an atmosphere filled with distrust.

> D is for dishonest.
> I is for intimidating.
> S is for self-serving.
> T is for tacky.
> R is for rude. This is an understatement.
> U is for uninterested in others.
> S is for skeptical or suspicious.
> T is for tricks and no treat.

The ineffective manager is very good for the pharmaceutical industry because of the health related issues that she may cause among employees. This manager creates an environment that causes headaches, anxiety, high blood pressure, nervousness, tension, and chronic stress. Perfectly healthy employees become unhealthy in the midst of the stress created by ineffective management. The only true perfection is the stress that is created and passed on to subordinates.

I am saddened when I notice employees develop sickly habits because of stress. Some employees stop exercising because they no longer have the time to commit to an exercise program. Their thirty-minute walks each day may no longer seem like an option. Nervous employees eat unhealthy snacks and grab unhealthy meals while they proceed to work at their desks. They consume large quantities of unnecessary calories. These unhealthy habits are created to relieve the tension and stress created by their managers.

An employee must take control of his health or an ineffective manager will destroy him. Take a day of personal leave each month. Pick a day when you won't worry about work. Watch a movie. Read a book. Plant a garden. Wash the car. Anything you choose to do will increase your feeling of control. The bottom line is to look after number one. A healthy employee is a productive employee.

The funding allocated to the agency suffers as much as the health of the employees. The taxpayers must shoulder the burden of ineffective and inefficient management. Funds are spent needlessly and foolishly at the whim of management. An example is when the goose lays a golden egg full of cash that must be spent by a certain deadline. The money magically appears as a result of the curious management of funds. The extracurricular money is casually referred to as rollover funds, line item funds, or grants. The pot of excess funds can be used for training or equipment. The magical key to the funds is the timing of expenditure. The money must be spent by a certain day or it will disappear as quickly as it appeared. Consequently, training sessions that are of no benefit to employees are provided in expensive hotels, equipment that will never be used is purchased, and trainers from the private sector make a truckload of cash in a short period of time. This extraordinary phenomenon usually happens at the end of a fiscal year due to some mysterious management of funds.

There will be negative consequences for ignoring ineffective and inefficient management. The ineffective manager will assume that creating an environment of distrust and negativity will enhance the performance of the work unit. The manager will assume that his leadership style is a welcome relief to clients and taxpayers. He will respond negatively to those who confront his style and approach. He is an expert at using information and circumstances to dethrone subordinates who practice honest measures and have integrity. A subordinate cannot be too careful when he finds himself led by an ineffective manager. Exposing the ineffective manager will be a slow and drawn-out process because the manager has already convinced his superior that he has the best interest of all parties in mind.

Proceed with caution when you find yourself confronted with an ineffective manager who is vindictive and retaliatory. The brewing storm can be controlled and subdued, but the effort is akin to finding a crocodile in the everglades and killing him with a kitchen knife. The ineffective manager is in a comfortable environment with maximum control whereas the unfortunate subordinate is in an uncomfortable environment with minimal control. The situation should not be ignored because the consequences of ignoring the destruction of ineffective management will be on the magnitude of an EF5 tornado.

The ineffective manager has one fear. She fears she will be exposed as a bully by her subordinates. State government has no place for the bully or the storm. Taxpayers are not willing to spend their dollars on such poor management. The bully should be exposed for the environment she has created. The best route is to confront the bully in an ethical and professional manner.

If you are in this situation, contact your human resources department and ask about filing a grievance. A grievance will force an investigation into the behaviors of the ineffective manager. Make certain that you have witnesses to the abusive behavior and that the witnesses will support your observations. Keep e-mails and memos that reflect a negative approach to management. Keep a record of conversations when the manager makes one statement and yet does something different. Keep a record of broken promises.

The human resources department of an organization is obligated to respond to complaints of favoritism, harassment, sexual harassment, discrimination, or any other intentional wrongdoing on the part of managers or anyone else in the organization. The human resources department also must maintain confidentiality and remain impartial. Get to know the members of your human resources department. Become comfortable with engaging them with questions about survival tactics.

Bully managers do not last forever; it only seems like they do. You will have nothing to fear if you remember what your mother told you when you were in kindergarten: Keep your nose clean. She meant it literally when you were five. I mean it figuratively today. Keep the principals that you know to be good:

1. Treat others like you want to be treated.
2. Be respectful of the organization and its policies.
3. Be courteous to your customers.

> "Adversity is like a strong wind. It tears away from us all but the things that cannot be torn, so that we see ourselves as we really are."
>
> Arthur Golden
> *Memoir of a Geisha*

RAINBOW
AN EFFECTIVE EMPLOYEE DESTINED FOR MANAGEMENT

A rainbow is a reminder that a storm is over. It has a multitude of colors, red, orange, yellow, green, blue, indigo, and violet that combine to form something visionary in the sky. An employee who has the skills and ability to be promoted into management is similar to the vision of a rainbow. Like the colors in the rainbow, he has seven highly desirable traits.

Do you have what it takes to be a manager in state government? What makes an employee valuable to the organization? An employee who brings happiness and joy to the workplace is an employee who can perform the essential functions of his position and is respectful of the terms and conditions of employment. He accepts additional responsibilities when called upon. He learns quickly and adapts to a changing environment. He follows direction and welcomes constructive criticism. He smiles, dresses appropriately, and interacts appropriately with coworkers and customers.

Employees with potential management skills have seven traits that are easily recognized by management. The Seven C Test may accelerate the process of identifying an excellent employee. Just like the colors of a rainbow, a talented employee has seven traits that start with the letter C.

1. **Competent:** The employee has the skills and knowledge to perform the essential functions of the position.

She requires very little training and hits the ground running. She is productive within the first few months of orientation.

2. **Congenial:** The employee is friendly and gets along with other employees. She wears a pleasant expression and is courteous to customers. She is willing to help cowork- ers and is responsive to the questions and concerns of customers.

3. **Consistent:** The employee is emotionally stable and has the same demeanor day after day. She does not fret or complain. A manager never has to worry about an inap- propriate outburst from this employee.

4. **Careful:** The employee works cautiously and depend- ably. She does not make many mistakes. She is quick to correct the few mistakes she makes. She understands office politics and community politics. She represents the agency well at any function.

5. **Credible:** The employee has credibility with her coworkers and customers. Others believe her explana- tions for processes and procedures. She is honest and trustworthy.

6. **Courageous** – The employee strives to make the right decisions and do the right things. He refrains from lis- tening to office gossip, making negative comments, and stealing time from the agency on the Internet or phone. He does not attempt to be liked by all employees.

7. **Competitive** – The employee competes with himself and with other employees in a fair and positive manner. He strives to become more proficient in everything that

he does. He is not satisfied to simply be average. He works diligently to be the best that he can be.

An employee with management skills is thoughtful of other employees. He is responsive to employees who are on sick leave or are facing crises. He demonstrates a desire to help with work and promotes a spirit of camaraderie within his office. He thinks of reasons to celebrate the accomplishments of coworkers. He remembers birthdays and special events.

An employee destined for management demonstrates a unique ability to interact appropriately with his respective supervisor. He follows a very simple code of conduct when he meets with his supervisor.

1. **He makes an appointment.** The effective employee assumes his boss is busy and makes an appointment. He does not take unnecessary time talking about his weekend or plans for dinner. He is on time for the appointment and has his thoughts organized. He is prepared and is concise with his presentation.

2. **He uses his time wisely.** He does not fidget or get comfortable in the supervisor's office. He does not take anything to drink or eat while he is in his supervisor's office. He understands that many employees and customers need some time alone with the boss.

3. **He remains positive no matter the outcome of the meeting.** He never shows disappointment or anger over decisions that are made. He is patient and understands that there will be another opportunity to make his presentation.

4. **He respects his boss whether he deserves it or not.** It may be disheartening to work for an incompetent supervisor, but this too will pass. The incompetent supervisor was selected for his position by someone else. An employee must put up with it until changes are made.

Employees who are selected for management have oftentimes been confidants to other managers. A good confidant is trustworthy and honest. She has the best interest of the agency at heart and mind. She does not betray her manager and offers sound advice when asked to do so. I have never known a manager who did not have a confidant.

1. **A confidant is trustworthy.** You can trust her with confidential information. She does not share confidential information with other employees. She keeps the information confidential unless the manager provides other instructions.

2. **A confidant is respected by coworkers.** No one wonders why a confidant is chosen. Other employees notice the same positive characteristics and understand the logic of selecting this individual. She has excellent command of policy and procedures. Coworkers ask for her opinion on a regular basis.

3. **A confidant is a consummate professional.** She dresses appropriately. She interacts appropriately with others. She observes the terms and conditions of employment. She is at work on time, stays on task, and works a minimum of eight hours per day. She does not abuse sick

leave and requests annual leave in advance. She makes the agency look good wherever she goes.

4. **A confidant will not take advantage of a friendship.** She will never brag about the relationship or use the relationship to gain leverage with other staff. She understands that her place is special; however, she never uses her status to gain anything for herself. She will not make the boss uncomfortable by asking for perks or favors.

5. **A confidant will disagree with her supervisor in a respectful manner.** She will be the one person who will tell the supervisor when he has made a mistake. The confidant is aware of office politics and provides a plethora of information for the supervisor.

A talented employee is not satisfied to simply work eight hours per day. He gives back to his professional organization and to his community. He may be active in his church, fraternity, sorority, or a civic organization. He seeks avenues outside of work to develop his leadership skills.

An employee with a majority of the skills discussed in this chapter will be on a fast track to management. It becomes easy to identify these employees because they exhibit the cherished traits of effective and efficient managers.

RED FLAG WARNING
HIRE WITH CAUTION

A manager has the responsibility to hire the right person for the job. The employee selection process is one of the most critical functions of a manager. Hiring an individual who cannot or will not perform the essential functions of the job causes a managerial nightmare. The last problem a manager needs is a body who takes up space and robs the office of air. Employees who cannot perform the essential functions of a position are an annoyance and a nuisance. It is preferable to have an empty cubicle or office. The financial burden of hiring the wrong person can be astronomical. You may as well hire a bear to work at your agency.

The consequences of hiring an employee who cannot perform the essential functions of the job are far reaching and have a dramatic impact on the agency for years to come. An ineffective or incompetent employee costs the agency and the taxpayers additional training dollars. He does not learn the basics of the job during orientation and training, and so the employer is forced to provide remedial or refresher training. The front-line manager is ultimately responsible for the mistakes of the incompetent employee. Coworkers become angry and resentful because they are asked to compensate for the mistakes that are made by the incompetent employee. Office morale plummets. Customers begin to complain loudly because they are not receiving quality services from the agency. In these ways, the incompetent employee will cost the taxpayers a small fortune.

Hiring the wrong person for the job sends the wrong message to customers and coworkers. First, it demonstrates that the manager does not have the judgment or experience required to excel in the interview and hiring process. Coworkers must absorb the duties that the incompetent employee is unable or unwilling to perform. Coworkers must try to make some sense of the predicament and may assume the individual is a political gift. A political gift is an individual who has connections to politically powerful persons who can persuade managers to hire someone lacking the necessary skills and experience. However, it has been my experience that most incompetent employees do not have political associations. They simply got lucky and fooled the employer during the interview process.

There are steps that can be taken to ensure you do not hire an employee who cannot perform the essential functions of the position.

1. **Be wary of reference checks.** Other employers will dump incompetent employees if given the opportunity. The present manager may provide a good reference so that he does not have to be bothered with disciplinary action and the rigorous protocol that precedes termination. Do not contact personal references. A personal reference usually knows very little about the individual's ability to perform essential functions, his work ethic, or his punctuality. The personal reference has no experience with the individual in an employment setting.

2. **Select the right coworkers to work on the interview questions and interview team.** A really good interview

takes as much prep time prior to the interview as during and following the interview. Pick coworkers who possess the skills and work ethic you are seeking in a new hire. Design questions that will get the answers necessary to make the decision. Select coworkers who will make a positive impression on the applicants.

3. **Take time to make the right decision.** The job did not become vacant for no reason. Think about the individual you want to hire. Remain alert during the interview. Watch the mannerisms of the individual. Record all the dialogue. Pay attention to any negative remarks. Keep in mind that an individual who speaks negatively about his present employer will speak negatively about his next employer. Observe his behavior and body language. It's normal to be nervous during an interview. However, an applicant who displays excessive nervousness through body language should be avoided. There is often a profound reason for the nervousness.

4. **Do not become desperate to fill the position.** You may feel pressure from coworkers or your boss. Customers may have complained about the lack of responsiveness from the agency. You may assume all your problems are related to a vacant position. A manager can and should learn to be patient. Patience is a virtue in this instance. An empty cubicle is not a problem. Develop patience and you will find your treasure.

5. **Listen to your instincts.** Follow your instincts. Never persuade an individual to take a job. It will backfire. If you have reservations about an individual, there is a reason for the concern. Recognize and obey your instincts. A manager's instincts about applicants are developed

over time and with experience. Accept that an applicant may not be right for the job if she is hesitant to accept your offer of employment. Her instincts may be telling her it's not a good match. Accept it and move forward to the next applicant.

You may follow all these steps and still find that you have hired the wrong person. What can you do if you find yourself with the wrong person? You can't force him to leave. You can't starve him. He gets paid whether he can do his job or not. You can't harass him in any way. He has more rights than you do. You can't trick him into leaving. That would not be ethical and could backfire. The incompetent employee is protected by employer policies, the Equal Employment Opportunity Commission, and the Americans with Disabilities Act if he has a disability.

Embrace the fact that you may be stuck with the incompetent employee for a very long time. Most incompetent employees do not leave the feeding trough unless forced to do so. The employee has a steady meal ticket and is content to remain at the trough until another food source is introduced. Most incompetent employees do not recognize that they cannot adequately perform the essential functions of their position. Contact your human resources department the minute you realize you have a problem with an employee's performance. Start working with the individual to correct the problems. Document all meetings with the individual. You will have an opportunity to dismiss the problem employee in the first year of employment in most government agencies. It is your window of opportunity. Most agencies refer to this window of time as the working test or probationary period for new or recently promoted employees. It is critical to monitor performance during the first year by regularly observing the individual and checking her actual work assignments.

An effective manager must develop coaching techniques. Coaching is necessary when the manager perceives a need for improvement. Coaching employs a complex set of techniques to help an individual achieve his potential. A manager should look for discrepancies between desired and actual performance. The discrepancies should be documented by the manager. Realistic goals and timelines should be noted in a short period of time. Regular meetings with constructive advice will enable the manager to determine if an employee is salvageable.

Be patient. Stay in contact with your human resources department. An incompetent employee can cause significant problems if the manager fails to follow protocol. Eventually the incompetent employee will find another source of food and shelter. You may be able to transfer the individual if he perceives he will not complete the working test.

Learn from your mistake. Resolve that it will never happen again. Learn to embrace the air, the empty seat, the phone that does not get answered, and the sounds of silence. It could be worse. The air and the silence will not hurt anyone. The empty seat will not steal your valuable time with questions and complaints. It could be worse. You could have a hungry bear in the cubicle or office.

Do not allow the employee to steal your joy. You will be tempted to forget about your other employees because you may become consumed with the incompetent employee. Focus on the employees who are performing their duties and responsibilities. I have witnessed many situations where managers become obsessed with negative employees and allow them to steal time from productive employees. A general rule of thumb to remember for management in state government is that on any given day you will have incompetent employees, average employees, and excellent employees. The data is usually broken into the following percentages:

10–15 percent are incompetent employees.

65–75 percent are average employees.

10–15 percent are excellent employees.

Give the average and excellent employees the attention they deserve. If you focus your energies on the incompetent employee, you will risk developing a negative attitude toward your work and other employees. You must be vigilant about keeping a positive attitude and presenting a positive image to the public.

TIDAL WAVE
DROWNING IN PAPER

A person begins his employment in state government with no money, and he ends his employment in state government with little money. You will need to invest your money wisely. Find fifty acres and grow some pine trees. Pine trees produce paper. Who ever thought computers would do away with paper? Remember when we were going to be a paperless society? We have never made it to that promised land. We have more paper today than ever before. The excessive use of paper in government offices is phenomenal. Offices are flooded with paper, and a manager cannot escape the avalanche of paper. A paper trail will follow him to the moon and back.

Why do we need so much paper? Offices are forced to increase space not because of new employees but because of paper. Government offices are littered with paper. We have copier paper, printer paper, folders, calendars, certificates, notebooks, pads, toilet paper, newspapers, magazines, index cards, paper towels, napkins, and tissues. We have rolls of paper, reams of paper, stacks of paper, and paper that needs to be shredded. We have folders in red, green, blue, and manila. Paper use is an industry.

We copy everything. Not once but twice. We send one copy to the supervisor, one to the director, and keep the other one to prove we sent the copies. Sometimes a client wants a copy of his record. We keep hard copies in the event a computer crashes and loses everything. We house hard paper copies for three years, five years, and seven years, depending upon the program.

Some government agencies do not spend the necessary money or do not have the funds to ensure the agency has the proper computer equipment to support the work of the agency. Some computer systems are slow, not dependable, and create the need for paper copies of everything. A computer program for client services that is difficult to operate and not dependable will ensure that employees make paper copies of everything. A conscientious employee will make two copies of everything.

Protect yourself with a paper trail. Are you having problems with a subordinate? Tackle the problem with paper. The winner will be the one with the most paper. Documentation is the key. Most information will be in your computer; however, you want to be sure you can retrieve it and hold it in your hands. There is a certain amount of security when you hold some paper with words on it. The paper is a source of comfort.

Keep documentation of your achievements and accomplishments. Your supervisor will change frequently if you are a line or middle manager. You will be asked to provide documentation of your value to the agency when it's time for the annual performance appraisal. This will be the one and only time that it will be acceptable to boast about your performance with as much words and paper as possible.

Presentations and training sessions are additional opportunities for paper. Hold the paper and you know you will present the information on the paper well. Look at the paper and you will learn from the presenter. Each participant will need a copy of the presentation. Participants watch PowerPoint presentations and receive a paper copy to keep at their desks. An agenda must be typed and provided for each participant. A printed agenda must be attached to travel statements to ensure you had a reason to travel.

An agency may require multiple layers of paper for travel reimbursement. Reimbursement for employee overnight travel can be a nightmare. It may take five weeks for a state employee to receive reimbursement. The employee may have to pay interest on his credit card because of the time it takes to receive the reimbursement. The employee is required to include the hotel receipt with a zero balance, program agendas, and multiple signatures. The travel request is sent to Atlanta for more signatures, and eventually it may land on the desk of an employee who may find insignificant errors and delay the reimbursement by asking for additional verification. Additional verification always translates to additional paper.

Find even more opportunities for paper use. A case record in a government office may grow to one inch every year depending upon the complexity of the case. The application may grow to ten pages depending upon the type of case. Medical or psychological documentation may be required to determine eligibility and assessment for a plan of services. Economic eligibility must be determined. Case notes are maintained in the computer system but are routinely copied for case convenience.

Case records are checked by auditors. The auditor requires an additional copy of each record. Case reviews are performed each month by supervisors and the supervisor's supervisor. The case review report is approximately ten pages. A client may request a copy of his record. Case record information is shared with other organizations if clients permit this exchange of information.

Personnel files with performance issues increase the value of stocks in paper production companies. Documentation, documentation, documentation, and more documentation is the order of the day for the progressive discipline process. The process starts with a simple confrontation, which must be documented by the supervisor. Each meeting must be recorded, and follow-up must be documented on the progress the individual is making to improve his performance. Several weeks or months of meetings and documentation may determine that the individual must be terminated. Finally, the proposal to dismiss is presented to the individual. The dismissal proposal may lead to a hearing, which will require additional documentation.

Keep tissues for employees who get emotional for one reason or another. A confrontation with an employee who is not performing the essential functions of the job is an excellent opportunity for various types of paper products. The manager will need to document the session and provide copies for the employee, human resources, the supervisor, and the manager's records. The employee may become emotional and start crying. The manager can offer a tissue to the employee. Hopefully, this will appear thoughtful and genuine.

Tissues can be used for allergies that are aggravated by environments that are unhealthy. I have worked in offices that were not properly maintained by the landlord. The roofs leaked each time it rained. The ceiling tiles were usually wet, and the carpet was occasionally wet. Mold grew in the offices faster than Bermuda grass grows in the summer. If you do not have allergies when you begin employment with state govern-ment, you may be afforded multiple opportunities to develop allergies because of environmental issues that exist in some offices.

Toilet paper is consumed in large quantities in a govern-ment office. Female employees use the facilities all day long. We require bathroom tissue for everything we do. I really don't know much about men. Women go to the john all day. Some women have overactive bladders. Some women have monthly problems that require multiple trips to the restroom. Some employees drink too much coffee or too many soft drinks. The results are the same. The consumption of fluids causes multiple trips to the restroom and the need for rolls of tissue.

Invest your money wisely. Invest in the paper industry. Plant pine trees and watch them grow. You can relax and know that your investment may find a home in a government office.

CAUTION
TALK AT YOUR OWN RISK

The tongue can be a manager's best asset, or it can be a manager's biggest enemy. The choice is yours to make. There are Biblical verses that express this gospel better than I can. The Biblical verses are powerful testimonies to the powers of the tongue. A loose tongue is as difficult to tame as the direction of the wind. The wind blows and leaves a path of debris and ugliness. Wind can forever change the appearance of the environment. The almighty tongue can forever change the upward direction of a career in state government. Scriptures are recorded in The Holy Bible, New International Version; Copy right 1984 by the International Bible Society.

> **James 3:5: Likewise the tongue is a small part of the body, but it makes great boasts. Consider what a great forest is set on fire by a small spark.**

The tongue is the most powerful muscle in the body. It is the only muscle that is not attached at both ends. Its size, strength, and that one loose end make it a good symbol of the challenge of our speech. It can destroy a child. It can inspire a teenager. The tongue is the most significant tool a manager will use. Tame your tongue. Use it wisely. You have a choice. Your tongue can be your lifesaver and the best asset you have. Or your tongue can be your greatest liability and can become a weight chained to your ankle.

Know when you should listen and when you should speak. It is advantageous to develop listening skills. A quiet demeanor indicates to others that you are thoughtful about the decisions you make. A quiet demeanor is often associated with intellect and analytical skills. It is better to be silent than to speak and live to regret the words that flow from your mouth. Silence can be golden.

**Proverbs 14:7: Stay away from a foolish man,
for you will not find knowledge on his lips.**

The talkative or spontaneous tongue will make its owner appear too playful and undedicated. This tongue is chatty and offers few words of wisdom. The talkative tongue can place its owner in harm's way by being overly friendly and disinterested in the work of the organization. This tongue makes too many mistakes. It gets too up close and personal about private issues.

The spontaneous tongue can be an advantage in a setting that provides networking opportunities. The natural ability to meet and greet the public is sometimes referred to as the gift of gab. Learn to use your tongue wisely if you are blessed with the gift of gab. It can be a positive asset when used to speak to strangers and acquaintances. You can make acquaintances and encourage business relationships. A conference is an excellent networking opportunity to utilize the gift of gab. A manager can make the spontaneous tongue a professional asset. Train it to meet the right professionals who will advance your agency and career.

James 1:26: If anyone considers himself religious and yet does not keep a tight rein on his tongue, he deceives himself and his religion is worthless.

The critical tongue can get a manager in plenty of hot water. It is mean-spirited and harmful to employees and customers. The critical tongue can destroy the self-confidence of qualified employees. It can be harmful to customers who need services from the organization. It can incite and infuriate a customer. It does not pay to be overly critical of subordinates or superiors. The critical tongue makes an employee angry and less likely to do his job. A manager's critical tongue will not inspire an employee. Words of contempt will not motivate an employee. It does not pay to assume someone is lazy, irresponsible, ignorant, or corrupt.

You can never repair the damage caused by a loose tongue. It is impossible to clean the mess once the venom is spewed. You cannot grab the words or remove them from someone's head or heart. The words are carved in stone. Whoever said that sticks and stones may break your bones but words will never hurt clearly did not have a brain or a heart. Words do hurt. Words can cause considerable damage to the speaker and the target audience.

The wise tongue offers an entirely different reaction. Words of encouragement can be equally compelling to the intended recipient. Constructive criticism is a form of coaching that can correct inefficiency and ineffectiveness. It takes more time to be thoughtful and constructive; however, the investment of time is worth the outcome. The employee will appreciate your sensitivity and kindness. She will listen to your words. She will offer solutions to problems. Constructive criticism will increase loyalty to the organization. It can promote a healthy and positive attitude for the employee.

An opportunity to learn is presented when a mistake or error in judgment is made. Words that are delivered in a thoughtful and comprehensive manner can be a great opportunity to educate the employee. A mistake or error is an opportunity to educate and learn. Mistakes and errors become problematic when they are repeated. The opportunity to coach and educate should be when the mistake first occurs. Much time can be wasted if the manager does not address the problem verbally when he first notices the problem. Solutions to problems should be identified immediately. It becomes more difficult to correct the behavior the longer that it is repeated. The incorrect behavior that causes a mistake will become a habit. The only work-related habit that is positive is a habit that is effective and efficient.

Words of encouragement can produce habits that are productive and effective. Words can be used as positive reinforcement. Positive reinforcement is a technique used to encourage a desirable behavior. It is also called positive feedback. In this technique, the employee receives encouraging and favorable communication from another person. Positive reinforcement appears to work well for professionals. Words can be used to encourage the behavior that is productive and desirable. However, this management style can be counterproductive if you have an employee who is not learning her job at an acceptable pace. A manager must balance positive reinforcement with constructive criticism.

Punishment is used to weaken a behavior because a negative condition is introduced or experienced as a consequence of the behavior. Forms of punishment used by ineffective managers may include humiliation by calling attention to worker errors during a group meeting. Addressing a subordinate in an excessively loud voice may be viewed as punishment. The use of outdated or inappropriate terminology that is politically incorrect also may be viewed as a form of punishment.

Proverbs 15:1: A gentle answer turns away wrath. But a harsh word stirs up anger.

Communication is the key to excellent management. Any form of communication should be done through thoughtful deliberation and concern for the other party. A manager may be tempted to use profanity or insults when talking to an employee. This is never productive and will get the manager into significant trouble through the grievance process. Your words have the same meaning whether you scream or simply speak. It is never appropriate to raise your voice even if the individual is hearing impaired. Just speak. That's all you have to do. Speak meaningful words and document the words you have spoken.

Share as much information as possible and be as transparent as possible. Make it a personal policy to never make comments you cannot defend in court. Subordinates will be loyal to a leader who does not hide the decision-making process. Subordinates will trust a leader who discloses all decisions and shares information. Mistakes will be easier to overcome if the manager is transparent.

Proverbs 25:11: A word fitly spoken is like apples of gold in pictures of silver.

Look for opportunities to offer words of encouragement and praise. There is always an employee who is doing something productive and effective. A manager who focuses on the positive behaviors of employees will be a healthier and better-adjusted individual. Positive communications make the employee feel physically well and happy. Positive communications produce chemicals in the mind that promote health and well-being.

The opposite effect will happen if a manager chooses to use negative communication and focuses on negative behaviors. As I've mentioned previously, it is unhealthy to focus on just the negative behaviors of employees. The manager who uses negative communication and focuses on ineffective behaviors will gradually become as unhealthy and unhappy as his employees. The manager may be prone to develop headaches, digestive problems, and muscle pain. His neck may become stiff and difficult to rotate. His back may force him to have poor posture. He may find it difficult to sit at his desk or during a meeting. His mind will wander, and he may become easily distracted.

Find time every day to engage in positive conversations with employees. Positive communications will encourage productivity and efficiency in employees. Positive communications will make the manager and her employees feel healthy and strong. Make it a goal to recognize an employee each day before nine in the morning. It will become a habit that will pay large dividends in the future. Talk to yourself. Say positive comments about your work, the organization, and your coworkers. Keep the bright side in mind.

Colossians 4:6: Let your conversation be always full of grace, seasoned with salt, so that you may know how to answer everyone.

Actions speak louder than words; however, words are extremely important to the credibility of a manager. Pay attention to your speech. It matters not that you may be willing to walk the extra mile if you use expletives in your speech or if you scream at your employees. The volume and tone of your speech can completely delete any significant work you may do. Be mindful of the words you speak, the tone of your voice, and the volume of your speech.

Verbal communication skills cannot be overrated. Managers must be able to communicate to individuals and groups. Effective verbal communication can be enhanced through training and feedback. Verbal communication skills can be learned. A manager may have to practice in front of a mirror or talk into a recorder to gain insight into the art of verbal communication.

> **James 1:19:** My dear brothers, take note of
> this: Everyone should be quick to listen, slow to
> speak, and slow to become angry.

This Biblical verse has many applications to our everyday activities as managers. Listen to customers, coworkers, and your boss. Think before you speak. You can't take back words once they are spoken. You may apologize, but the damage is done. Do not succumb to anger. Nothing positive will come from an angry outburst.

1. Learn to listen.
2. Think before you speak.
3. Leave the anger at home.

ROGUE WAVE
TEMPTATION AT WORK

The life of a manager in state government can be very lonely. Do not succumb to the temptation of the forbidden fruit or anything involving sexual liaisons with employees no matter how lonely or bored you may be. You may think an employee is sexy and attractive. The moments of excitement will end when you or the employee become weary of the sexual relationship. The discontent or weariness will not occur simultaneously. The end is never mutual or lateral. Someone will be emotionally devastated. One person will become weary of the relationship long before the other individual.

Even the appearance of an inappropriate relationship can be a distraction to coworkers. The newly acquired relationship may be innocent and platonic; however, coworkers may perceive it in a sinister manner. Coworker curiosity about the relationship will interfere with client services and the office environment. It is a manager's responsibility to ensure that subordinates focus their energy and resources on clients and the mission of the agency.

A relationship with the forbidden fruit is similar to a day that begins with sunshine and ends with a rogue wave. It is difficult to imagine that a beautiful beginning can end in destruction and chaos. A manager cannot help himself or protect himself from the final results of an inappropriate relationship. It will end with a certain level of disaster. An inappropriate relationship can end a career.

An inappropriate relationship can happen without warning. I have not known any manager who deliberately searched for an inappropriate relationship. In many instances, the manager was caught off guard. It usually starts with an innocent flirtation that is not intended to escalate. The manager and the employee know the relationship is not appropriate or ethical. It is the responsibility of the manager to prevent any physical contact. This is sometimes more difficult than it appears. The escalation into a full-blown affair is usually gradual. Neither the manager nor the employee realizes it has evolved into a relationship until it is too late. There are several avenues through which an affair with the forbidden fruit may occur.

The subordinate (employee) may initiate the relationship. This may appear to be safe; however, it can lead to the death of a career. The employee will start with an easy flirtation. It can be something as simple as fetching the morning newspaper or fixing the coffee. It may escalate with a compliment from the employee. There may be a mental or physical attraction. The employee may like the way the manager dresses, walks, or talks. The employee may think the manager is smart or sexy or smart *and* sexy. The subordinate develops a desire to be close to the boss. He initiates some activities that began the lonesome road to the illicit affair.

The seduction may have nothing to do with physical attraction. There may be a more sinister motive. The employee may perceive that the boss has the power to make his life easier and more lucrative. The chase is all about what the boss can do for the employee. It has nothing to do with physical attraction. The seduction is about money and power. Once the employee has more money or a new position, the employee will drop the relationship. The relationship will no longer serve a purpose. The manager may become angry and hurt. The manager may feel used and may react emotionally. It becomes important to maintain composure and not retaliate in any way. The hurt will eventually go away. A manager may be able to salvage his career if he plays it cool and allows the employee to fade away.

There are usually extenuating circumstances that lead to the moment of physical contact with a subordinate. The manager may be unhappy at home. He may be vulnerable. He may want more excitement in his life. The manager may be bored at work. The subordinate may pursue the unwilling manager until he can longer fight the desire to have physical contact. Any one of these circumstances will increase the likelihood that an affair will happen. The affair will relieve some symptoms in the beginning; however; the day will come when the affair only adds to the frustration of everyday life.

An inappropriate physical or emotional relationship in the office has a negative impact on coworkers. The relationship becomes tabloid fodder at work. It becomes a distraction. Coworkers begin spending time watching the subordinate and the manager. Coworkers talk about the relationship at break, by the water fountain, during meetings, and after hours. Coworkers may assume that the employee is receiving perks and extra benefits for the illicit relationship.

An inappropriate relationship damages a manager's relationship with other coworkers and subordinates. Coworkers may lose respect for the manager and the employee. Coworkers may use the information to create problems for the manager. Coworkers may take the information about the illicit affair to the manager's spouse or family. Coworkers may file a grievance citing favoritism.

The employee may file sexual harassment at the beginning or end of the relationship. Sexual harassment is taken very seriously by human resources. The allegations will be investigated by an outside resource. The investigation will disrupt work and other office functions. The determination of sexual harassment can be a subjective decision made by the investigator and based on observations by other employees. A guilty verdict can lead to demotion, suspension, or termination. It will not be pretty no matter what the results.

The bottom line is to resolve that you will resist the temptation to eat the forbidden fruit. It matters not what your home situation may be. It matters not how tempting the fruit may be. The affair will not last. The excitement will not last. The penalties and punishment for having an affair with a subordinate at work will last forever. You will also need to guard against creating the perception that you are having an inappropriate relationship. Both situations can consume valuable time and resources.

Take this message one step further and be cautious about friendships at work that extend beyond office hours. Any relationship with a subordinate after hours can trigger a complaint from a coworker. Coworkers may perceive that the subordinate receives benefits or does not have to abide by the terms and conditions of employment because of the relationship.

It is a manager's responsibility to manage the perception of inappropriate behavior at work. A manager lives on an island surrounded by dolphins and sharks. You can choose to swim with the dolphins; however, a shark will be watching and waiting for a bite of your flesh.

SWIM TO SHORE
INSPIRE YOURSELF

You will need to swim to shore when you are tempest tossed. You will know what an inspiration the Bible can be if you are a Christian. A Christian will be familiar with the Biblical books of Proverbs and James. There are verses in each book that are applicable to management and relationships at work. I have found these verses to be spiritually uplifting in times of indecision, encouraging in times of despair, and comforting in times of loneliness. Some verses have provided the necessary wisdom to make difficult decisions and the courage to stay the course. The words are reassuring and energizing. The words of the Lord offer comfort and support in a sea of uncertainty. Scriptures are recorded in The Holy Bible, New International Version, copyright 1984, by the International Bible Society.

Proverbs was written by Solomon. He was the son of David and is associated with wisdom. Each verse is applicable to daily circumstances and can be applied to our unique work circumstances. James was written by James, the disciple of Jesus Christ. There are numerous verses in James that are applicable to management and work relationships.

There are other books in the Bible that provide tips on leadership. Exodus is the story of Moses. Moses led the Israelites into the Promised Land. Moses was an introvert and did not aspire to be a leader. He had a problem with his speech. He was chosen by God just like so many leaders are chosen. He was hesitant about his role and tried to find reasons not to follow God's instructions. Ultimately, he did lead the Israelites into the Promised Land. He is one of my favorite leaders because of his reluctance and obvious flaws with interacting with people. Never the less, he followed instructions and completed his mission.

The Biblical books of Proverbs and James are incomparable in providing helpful information for managers. These books will lend clarity to your everyday challenges and questions. Read the first six verses of Proverbs and you will understand how important this Book is to managers.

> **Proverbs 1:1–6:** The proverbs of Solomon the son of David, king of Israel: for attaining wisdom and discipline: for understanding words of insight: for acquiring a disciplined and prudent life, doing what is right and just and fair: for giving prudence to the simple, knowledge and discretion to the young: let the wise listen and add to their learning, and let the discerning get guidance: for understanding proverbs and parables the sayings and riddles of the wise.

A wise manager knows that he does not know everything. He knows that he must embrace the fine art of learning. Effective managers make it a point to learn something new every day. Effective managers research topics to find answers to problems. Effective managers know who they can count on for quality information. Wise managers ask the right questions.

Know your area of expertise. No one is an expert on all topics. It is wise to develop knowledge and skills on a certain topic.

It makes one valuable to the organization. A manager is important to an organization when persons routinely refer others to him. Pick a topic that you love and that is meaningful to you.

Wise people surround themselves with other wise people. Wise people want to be in the same club, the same clique, or on the same team. Wise people are comfortable with one another. They complement one another. Wise people seldom find themselves with people who have few life experiences. A wise person will not spend time with people who cannot increase her level of understanding and knowledge.

Effective managers develop a keen ability to recognize and reward their coworkers who strive to learn all aspects of a position and as much about a company as possible. Wisdom does not come cheap. A manager will make some mistakes to gain the knowledge that is necessary to be declared wise. A manager must constantly seek wisdom. Most organizations have an abundance of intelligent employees but very few wise employees. A truly wise individual understands that he has never fully acquired wisdom. It is a trait he continually seeks.

Proverbs 3:27: Do not withhold good from those who deserve it, when it is in your power to act.

An effective manager recognizes that he has the power and responsibility to reward the workers who are critical to the success of the organization. Public managers cannot provide monetary rewards except in rare circumstances and at the end of the fiscal year. The effective manager must find alternate means to reward his star performers. It can be something as simple as a card or as complex as a trip to a national conference.

Never take your stars for granted. Begin every day with a series of compliments for coworkers who are performing at an optimal level. The praise can be in a simple form. Forward an e-mail that expresses appreciation. Write a note and place it in an employee's mailbox. Praise an individual or team at a company meeting. Provide opportunities for growth and development. Plan meetings and team building at sites away from the office. Designate choice parking spaces for the top employees. Make assignments that are rewarding.

An effective manager concentrates on coworkers who deserve her positive energy and attention. A manager should spend quality time with a star performer every day. The rewards are immeasurable. The excellent employee's star power will shine brighter when he knows he is appreciated and encouraged. He will grow exponentially. The reward to a manager who recognizes excellent work will be multiplied by the performance of the star individual. A manager must never underestimate the power of positive praise.

> **Proverbs 6–8:** Go to the ant, you sluggard: consider its ways and be wise! It has no commander, no overseer or ruler, yet it stores its provisions in summer and gathers its food at harvest.

An effective manager prays for the opportunity to work with a few good ants. Ants do their work, mind their business, and produce results. Ants do not overeat, drink too much, or take advantage of company breaks. Ants work as a team. They do not try to overshadow other ants, and they do not draw attention to themselves. The team with the most ants will be the team that succeeds. The effective manager will recognize the ants on his team for their consistency and dependability.

Proverbs 12:1: Whoever loves discipline loves knowledge. But he that hates correction is stupid.

Mistakes are opportunities to learn. An employee makes a mistake because she is doing something. An employee can't make a mistake if she relaxes and watches the time fly by. Sometimes an employee may receive a memo or lecture pertaining to a mistake she has made. An employee will accept the dose of medicine no matter how bitter it may be if the manager creates a learning objective. A defensive attitude will dissolve all efforts to learn from the experience. We should learn from our mistakes.

Allow employees the latitude to make a mistake. Ensure that the individual learns from the experience. She will be very unlikely to repeat the mistake. A mistake can open the door to clearer understanding. Consider it a training opportunity. Training opportunities provided by conferences or online courses are costly. It may be more cost-effective to learn from a mistake.

Proverbs 12:15: The way of a fool seems right to him, but a wise man listens to advice.

The ability and desire to listen and learn is perhaps the single best trait a manager can have. A manager who understands that he does not have all the answers is free to do research and ask others for advice. Don't assume that you have all the answers no matter how much experience you may have. It is my experience that the longer a manager plays the game, the less he knows. It is important to surround yourself with capable and smart coworkers. Seek their counsel and wisdom. Ask them to share their past experience with certain problems. You will find that several knowledgeable people can accomplish great things. You will be secure in the decision that you make if you have talked to the right people.

Proverbs 12:18: Reckless words pierce like a sword, but the tongue of the wise brings about healing.

Think before you speak. Angry words will not help any situation. They will cause the situation to escalate. A manager never needs to raise her voice or speak while angry. Prepare your presentation to employees. Be patient. Don't get sucked into speaking words that an employee will use against you. Keep in mind that a person who thinks he has done nothing wrong and never makes a mistake is a fool. You cannot reason with a fool. It will be counterproductive. The fool will use angry words when he files a grievance with human resources. Be kind. You can make the same points with words of wisdom that are softly spoken.

Proverbs 12:25: An anxious heart weighs a man down, but a kind word cheers him up.

You will encounter coworkers who are nervous and anxious. They may need medication; however, you cannot suggest that they see a physician because of the Americans with Disabilities Act. The anxious employee will spend hours criticizing his supervisor because he truly thinks the supervisor has caused his anxiety. Use kind words. Speak softly. The anxious coworker usually suffers a certain level of paranoia. He assumes the boss is out to get him. Thoughtful and considerate words will diffuse the situation. A manager can learn to make a point with soft and intelligent words.

Proverbs 13:18: He who ignores discipline comes to poverty and shame, but whoever heeds correction is honored.

We must accept discipline. It is a necessary part of management. We will make mistakes with our actions, budget, or case service funds. Mistakes can be corrected with the right attitude. Accept discipline from your supervisor. It will hurt less if you do not try to defend your actions. Be a loyal employee. Communicate to your boss that you will not repeat the mistake. Move forward. Think about what you learned from the counseling session or memo. Then move on. Keep moving forward and upward. Share that you have made mistakes with your employees. They will think you are human. It's good to be human when you work with humans.

Proverbs 14:29: A patient man has great understanding, but a quick-tempered man displays folly.

Anger is an emotion that should be left at home when you leave for work. It serves no purpose in the workplace. Anger is bad for the beholder for many reasons. An angry man cannot clearly reason with others. An angry man has a red face. An angry man has a wrinkled brow with lines etched around his mouth and eyes. An angry man has a heart that beats like he's running a marathon and may eventually cause health-related conditions such as high blood pressure and stroke. There are no physical benefits for an angry temperament. An angry man makes statements that are hurtful and cannot be retracted. Decisions that are made from anger are not right or ethical. An angry man seldom has all the facts. Anger reduces one's ability to think and reason. It also interferes with one's ability to compromise and find solutions that benefit all parties. Leave your angry emotions at home.

Use anger to make yourself healthier, smarter, and wiser. Program yourself to channel the anger into a positive emotion or action. Reduce the venom that flows in your blood through meditation, running, or swimming. Use medication as a last resort. Go to the gym for a brisk workout followed by a cold beer. The importance of this verse cannot be overstated. Do not allow your anger to make decisions or cause actions that will harm you. Anger can bite you like a snake.

Proverbs 20:13: Do not love sleep, lest you grow poor: stay awake and you will have food to spare.

A lazy manager is nonproductive. She reports to work later than other employees. She frequently leaves early in the afternoon. She calls in sick several times per year. Lazy managers cannot survive without energetic employees. The lazy manager is dependent upon her clerical staff to compensate for her lethargic behavior and inattentiveness. She does not lead by example but rather expects employees to cook the bacon and clean the house. A lazy manager does not return phone calls, does not respond to e-mails, and has a sloppy office. This type of behavior will eventually cause the manager to fail at major tasks. She will not check the work of others. Work may go incomplete for long periods of time. She will not become concerned until the lack of work is recognized by her supervisor. The lazy manager will then blame her employees and try to delegate her unfinished work.

You can avoid the temptation to become lazy. Rest well at night and exercise frequently. A brisk walk at lunch or in the afternoon will increase blood flow to the brain. Exercise will increase your chances for resting well at night. Strive to appear energetic at work. Energy and enthusiasm are contagious. Others will aspire to have energy and will work to get it.

NAVIGATING THE COURSE
THE EFFECTIVE AND EFFICIENT MANAGER

An effective and efficient manager is a navigator at sea for his coworkers, customers, and supervisor. He knows how to ride the waves whether the sea is tempest tossed or calm. This chapter is divided into three sections, Captain of the Ship, Lifeguard, and Storm Chaser. The Captain of the ship is responsible for his crew, the ship, and everything that occurs on a voyage. A lifeguard is responsible for the safety of his swimmers. He must stay fit and alert while on duty. A storm chaser must have courage and the mental stamina to determine the course of a storm and perform his duties.

Captain of the Ship

A manager is responsible for his subordinates, the public that his agency serves, and everything that takes place in the offices that he supervises. There are specific behaviors that a manager should employ while on duty. Effective managers can pass the E Test. You can determine that a manager is an effective navigator if he is effective, efficient, engaged, encouraging, and ethical.

1. **Effective:** An effective manager produces a desired effect or outcome. He sets goals and strives to produce a result that supports the mission of the agency. An effective manager communicates in a clear and concise

manner. He supports his staff and communicates goals and expectations. He reviews outcomes and indicators on a regular schedule. He notes the successful outcomes and provides guidance to subordinates who are not meeting expectations.

2. **Efficient:** An efficient manager can function without waste. He is capable of achieving the desired result with the minimum use of resources, time, and effort. He is frugal with travel funds and regular operating expenses. He watches out for the taxpayer. He manages his operating expenses as if the budget is his personal checking account. The efficient manager utilizes staff time appropriately. Meetings are planned and well organized. There is an agenda. The participants seldom get sidetracked. Every participant stays on task and completes the agenda in a timely manner. The efficient manager removes all barriers to productive performance.

3. **Engaged:** The engaged manager is committed to a cause that is bigger than self. He is greatly interested in subordinates and the agency. He makes it a point to know each subordinate. He knows their strengths and weaknesses. He knows how to motivate individuals and groups.

4. **Encouraging:** An encouraging manager will inspire with hope, courage, and confidence. He uses positive reinforcement to promote optimal effort. He concentrates on the positives and celebrates success with his subordinates. The encourager knows how to motivate subordinates. He treats subordinates like professionals.

5. **Ethical:** The primary values that serve as a foundation for this code include a commitment to the following:

a. Respecting human rights and dignity
b. Ensuring the integrity of all professional relationships
c. Acting to alleviate personal distress and suffering
d. Enhancing the quality of professional knowledge and its application to increase professional and personal effectiveness
e. Appreciating the diversity of human experience and culture
f. Advocating for fair and adequate provision of services

Managers who follow ethical principals clearly define and maintain ethical, professional, personal, and social relationships with subordinates and coworkers. An ethical manager avoids nonprofessional relationships with current subordinates or trainees.

The E Test is not easy to pass. Very few managers are effective, efficient, engaged, encouraging, and ethical. All additional characteristics can be built around the E Test. The taxpaying public deserves managers who can pass the E Test. Subordinates are loyal and comfortable with managers who pass the E Test. Customers are content and satisfied with managers who meet the E Test.

Effective managers come in all shapes, forms, and colors, but there are thirteen basic characteristics of the successful manager in state government. There may be others; however, the following characteristics are the ones I have observed the most.

1. **Adopt introvert behaviors.** Be introspective and thoughtful. Listen to others. Remain quiet and calm.

An introvert will remain calm when everyone around her is falling apart. Introverts are reflective and do not crave the limelight. Share the limelight with coworkers and bosses. Control your tongue and put it to work in a favorable way.

2. **Understand office politics.** Strive to understand the pecking order in the office. The effective manager can figure out who holds the power. Know the informal leaders. Informal leaders can provide valuable information to management. Informal leaders are usually liked and respected by most employees. The successful manager appears to be enemies with no one and friends with everyone.

3. **Understand state politics.** State politics can change every few years depending upon who receives the most votes. Respect and like all elected officials. It will serve no purpose to make a powerful enemy. You do not have to agree with the elected official. You just need to get along with all elected officials. I worked with an advocate for people with disabilities. She was a formidable political force. I learned that she didn't necessarily know or agree with all elected officials. Sometimes she opposed them strenuously. However, she made it a point to welcome any leader who made it to office. She found common ground with every elected official. This attitude paid many dividends for her agency.

4. **Be nimble and flexible.** Everything changes, and nothing remains the same. Accept this fact. Sometimes the sea is calm and the day is sunny. Sometimes you will be required to ride tidal waves and suffer through hurricanes. You may be asked to bend the rules for

a valuable employee who is experiencing a difficult personal situation. A flexible work environment will reduce the need for absenteeism and will increase the energy the employee can devote to work. Keep in mind that all seasons pass. Find something positive in every type of weather.

5. **Take nothing for granted.** Don't assume anything. It didn't happen if it's not documented. Always ask for a note or memo of clarification. Ask someone to take notes at each meeting. Send the notes to all participants and provide a deadline to respond if someone does not agree with the notes. Record each one-on-one meeting with staff members. Send a follow-up memo with the information so there is agreement on the contents of the meeting.

6. **Do not discuss salaries.** It will make you angry. There will always be an incompetent employee who makes more money than you do. It's foolish to fight over a salary. There are curious dynamics that have caused certain salaries to be small and others to be enormous. It can be something as simple as the year you were promoted. Or it can be something unchangeable like the year you were born. Discussion of salaries will make you physically and mentally ill.

7. **Wear a pleasant expression.** Everyone is watching you. Don't ever show concern or panic. Never let them see you sweat. Smile. A frown will cause undue concern and needless worry among employees. It will add wrinkles to your face. It will create an environment of doom and self-doubt. Coworkers will waste valuable company time trying to read your face and mind.

8. **Use correct grammar and enunciation.** This seems trivial, but you can appear unintelligent if you don't write and talk correctly. Use spell- check on e-mail and memos. Text using complete sentences and words. Make certain your text message is sent to the intended recipient. Someone will be watching.

9. **Take annual leave.** Annual leave will make you appear human. People will assume you have a life. You probably do not have a life; however, it is helpful to have the appearance of one. Go on a trip and talk about the fun you had. Make new friends and act as if you need a break from work. Refresh yourself on these sabbaticals. Look forward to your planned vacation time.

10. **Be of good cheer.** Laugh about your mistakes. Make light of the mistakes of others. Take cut flowers to the office. Read devotionals and inspirational words. Leave your emotions at home. No employee likes a manager who shows his emotions. It makes coworkers nervous and anxious. Stay in control of your emotions.

11. **Be kind to coworkers' children.** You will have the opportunity to be a positive influence on a young person. Your influence may have a far-reaching impact on the child and her future career. Kindness and consideration of others will promote loyalty to you and to the organization. Your coworkers will be indebted to you.

12. **Be a positive role model and mentor.** Someone is watching you. You have the unique opportunity to be a positive force in your office each day. It's easy to be

positive in the good times. It demonstrates character to remain positive in the bad times.

13. **Obey the terms and conditions of your employment.** Coworkers will appreciate your dedication. Lead by example. Act like you love your work. Find the positive reinforcement in all your activities. Get to work on time and leave work on time. Take periodic breaks that will renew your thought process.

Never let them see you sweat. Not figuratively or physically. The second is easier to master than the first. Simply wear deodorant and dress in layers. Cotton clothing is best since it will absorb the water. Don't stutter. Don't grind your teeth. Sip water or some other beverage throughout the day. A non caffeinated drink is best since the caffeine may cause your heart rate to increase. The following are a few suggestions and tips to consider to help you stay calm:

1. **Don't raise your voice.** Keep it at an even level. A monotone is better than a high-pitched churn or squeal. Remember that you can say no in the same voice that you can say yes. It is the terminology that is important. Your tone does not have to have significance unless you want it to be significant.

2. **Show no fear.** Be a lion at heart. You will occasionally be afraid. Never let your coworkers know that you are not confident. Move forward as if you trust your instincts. Don't fear making a mistake. You will make them. Embrace your mistakes as learning tools. What better method to learn than to make a mistake?

3. **Smile.** A smile will disarm your enemies and please your friends. It will make you feel better. A smile takes fewer muscles than a frown. You will look younger. A smile can be a healthy motivator. You may be forced to make routine dental appointments so that you can preserve your smile.

4. **Walk at a constant speed.** Don't slow down or speed up. Staff members will form their theories about the speed of your walk. If you walk too fast, they may assume there is an emergency. If you walk too slowly, they may assume you are unhappy with a managerial decision. You will decrease the possibility of tripping over an object, too.

5. **Pray daily.** Prayer and meditation are necessary for the healthy manager. They enrich your life and your ability as a manager. Read a daily devotional with a cup of java in the morning before you leave for work. Pray about every decision you make. Pray for friends and enemies. Pray for friends to have a good day and be successful. Pray for enemies to do no harm to you. Prayer works wonders. A prayer lifts the spirit and renews the strength.

Read and write. Write and read. You can never know enough. Learn something new every day. A good manager is cautious about what he writes. Anything written can come back to haunt a manager. A simple e-mail can devastate a career. A well-intended sympathy card can be construed as ethically incorrect and insulting. A nickname may be viewed as condescending or sexually provocative. Think before you write. You will see it again. Write as if you want the world to read it. Taking the necessary time to be proper and correct will be time well invested. You will not have to spend time in the future explaining your intentions.

E-mail has become one of the most common forms of communication. E-mail can be a very powerful tool. But remember to use some etiquette. Use e-mail in a customer-friendly manner. Begin e-mails with a greeting that is professional and courteous. A friendly greeting sets the pace and assures the recipient that you have good intentions. The recipient will read and digest the e-mail better if it begins in a friendly manner. You are addressing a fellow government employee, not a friend, enemy, or lover. Think before you write, and write accordingly.

Use bold print sparingly. Eyes automatically train themselves on the bold print. The content of the e-mail may be lost with the use of bold print. The intent of the note will be lost if there is too much bold print. It has the same impact as screaming at the recipient. Respect your e-mail recipient.

End the e-mail with your name. It only takes two seconds to sign your name or tap the name, address, and title return key. The recipient will feel like you think of him as a person and not just an employee. You will improve communications and relationships significantly.

Use the ostrich approach sometimes. There will be situations where you may want to take the ostrich approach and bury your head in the sand. Go ahead and do it. The ostrich approach will buy time to learn the facts, analyze the situation, and form some solutions. Sometimes this may be your best solution to problematic situations. Do not use the ostrich approach on a full-time schedule, though. You will want to be seen and heard in most situations. Reserve this extreme behavior for the rare times when there is no immediate solution.

Lifeguard

A lifeguard on the beach must be physically and mentally fit to perform the duties of his job. A manager should be physically and mentally fit for similar reasons. The effective manager has his priorities in order. No person can be successful without recognizing the importance of prioritizing one's life. The effective manager will follow three rules for mental and physical well being.

1. **Take care of yourself.** An effective manager must stay physically, emotionally, and mentally healthy. Make your physical and mental needs a priority each day. You can't take care of your job, your family, or anyone else if you don't take care of you. Exercise each day. Walk to work. Take the stairs. Ride a bike. Go to the gym. You don't have to overwhelm your body or your head. Moderate or mild exercise is beneficial. It will clear your head and increase your blood flow. This will increase your ability to think and reason. It will enhance your ability to make decisions that are effective and efficient. You will look better and feel better. Exercise will give you a boost in self-confidence and self-esteem. A touch of discipline will make you appear dedicated and in control of your domain. Exercise will greatly reduce your chances of developing diabetes, high blood pressure, and obesity. You will be able to better control any disease you may have rather than allowing the disease to control you. Visit your dentist

regularly. Brush your teeth and use mouthwash. Use dental floss. People will like you more if you look and smell your best.

Take time for you. Read something you enjoy. Drink hot tea or cappuccino. Join a civic group or organization. Attend church. Read a devotional. Volunteer for community events. Watch a movie. Stand on your head. Punch the air. Do anything that is legal and makes you feel alive.

Stay home when you are not well. Your road to recovery will be shorter if you rest for a few hours or a few days. You will set an example for your coworkers. They will get the impression that you care about them and do not want to risk passing your illness on to them. A day alone at home will clear the cobwebs from your head. It will refresh your body. You will find that you have solved problems without thinking about the problems. The office will survive without you. Questions you would have answered will be answered by someone else. Your unexpected absence will cause other leaders to grow and develop. Enjoy your brief illness.

2. **Take care of your family and friends.** As a manager, you will not be able to concentrate on work if you are thinking about your family. Spend time with your children and their friends. Call a friend. Take time for ballgames, school plays, recitals, and other family activities. Take a vacation. Stay home with your children when they are ill. Take them to the physician. Meet your spouse for lunch. Let them know they are first and primary in your life. Act like you don't care about going to work if they need you.

3. **Take care of your job.** Your job affords you the opportunity to live in a house and neighborhood. Your job buys the car, pays the health insurance, pays the gym fee, and pays college tuition. Treat it with respect. Don't take your job for granted. It can disappear. Go to work with a cheerful attitude. You will feel better and you will look better.

My Methodist minister compared the priorities of life in this manner. You have five balls. The balls represent work, health, family, friends, and faith. The ball that is work is rubber. You can drop it and it will bounce. In other words, you will always have work to do. There will always be unfinished work. The other balls are glass and breakable. You may not have a second chance with the other balls.

Meetings are another challenge for effective management. Some public managers do not know how to start or end meetings. Some meetings have no purpose and contain little meaningful activity. Little consideration is given for the salary of the employee who spends countless hours in meetings or the costs of lodging, meals, and mileage. It is a sad state of affairs for taxpayers who unwillingly fund these activities. There are a few coping mechanisms that will allow you to endure meetings that start at dawn and end at dusk with no purpose in mind.

1. Take aspirin or another over-the-counter painkiller before and after the meeting.

    A mild painkiller will reduce the possibility of developing a severe headache. It will decrease muscle spasms that occur because of sitting in one position for hours.

2. Drink gallons of water and juice. The liquids will keep your body hydrated. You won't be as likely to develop a headache.

3. Fidget and squirm in your chair. Wiggle your toes. The movement will cause increased blood flow. Clench your fists and cross and uncross your legs. Your blood flow will increase cranial activity, and you will make better decisions.

4. Take advantage of breaks. Go to the restroom or vending stand. The walk will rejuvenate you. You may even see a friend.

5. Eat snacks, but never eat large meals. A large meal will cause drowsiness. Snacks will invigorate you and will provide a small reward while you sit and listen.

6. Daydream. Think about retirement. Create your bucket list.

7. Act like your sinuses are bothering you and leave the room for a brief period. Grab a tissue when you return to the room. Act like you are having problems with your nose. People will sympathize with your illness.

8. Stay alert with caffeine. The caffeine will prevent you from sleeping at inopportune times.

9. When all else fails and you can take it no longer, tell the participants that you have diarrhea. No one will ask for details, and everyone will hope you go home.

Develop a healthy sense of humor. Reduce the likelihood of negative reactions and responses. Laughter is good for the soul and the body. It can diffuse a hostile environment. Incorporate humor in all your meetings. Laughter causes your body to release endorphins. Coworkers will appreciate you.

Develop the stamina to stay the course. Decisions will be made that you do not agree with. Channel your energy into a productive mode to change a wrong decision or transaction. Don't be paralyzed by the inappropriate action. Do something positive about it. Purge negativity in a proper manner. Failure to manage negative feelings may cause you to develop a health problem that will consume you mentally and physically. A health problem caused by stress at work will destroy you if it is allowed to grow and multiply. It will zap your energy and cause serious illnesses. High blood pressure, diabetes, obesity, and anxiety disorder can be directly related to stress at work.

Stress is a leading cause of the release of the chemical cortisol in the bloodstream. Over time this chemical can be harmful to your body. It will accelerate the aging process. Don't allow the offending behavior or cancer to control your life. Take the proper steps to find the appropriate course of action. Manage stress through diet and exercise. Eat a healthy diet rich in vegetables and fruits. Maintain a proper weight. A healthy diet should contain protein, complex carbohydrates, water, and vitamins.

Limit alcohol and caffeine consumption. Some alcohol may be advantageous to your health. If you choose to drink alcohol, drink responsibly. Monitor the amount you consume. Too much alcohol may lead to an alcohol-induced headache. It may cause you to make decisions that are not in your best interest. Operating a vehicle while intoxicated or buzzed can lead to much larger headaches and large monetary expenditures on attorney fees and fines. It can be career ending if you happen to harm someone while you are operating a vehicle. Caffeine can give you a physical and psychological boost. However, too much caffeine may cause you to be nervous and jittery.

Exercise thirty minutes per day. Do not let this be an option. Make it an important part of your day. Carve out the time for it. Work exercise into your daily schedule. Morning, noon, or night is fine. Walking is great. You will be surprised to find some solutions for your issues while you are exercising. You may complete your exercise routine only to find that you know the answer to a problem.

Put funds aside to pay for snacks and recognition. A position in management in state government will cost you a lot of money. It is an expectation that managers attend luncheons to honor birthdays, retirements, and other occasions. In addition to luncheon attendance, a small contribution will be expected from your meager paycheck. You will be ostracized as being cheap and unsupportive if you do not make a contribution. You have no choice but to spend at least $10 on lunch. If you do lunch once a week for the year, you will spend $480.

The manager is responsible for snacks, water, and coffee at meetings. The costs add up. Suppose you have monthly meetings, and there are 15 employees who participate in the meetings. You may spend a minimum of $3 per individual. This expenditure will be $45 per meeting and will add up to $540 per year. I know of no tax deductions for this expenditure.

Storm Chaser

A storm chaser is courageous and determined in his quest to track a storm. He makes every effort to understand the path of a storm; consequently, he must learn as much about the storm as possible. A manager must know as much as possible about his subordinates, other managers, and anyone with whom he may have business. It pays to understand why decisions are made and to understand why persons react to certain circumstances. A manager must develop courage to make appropriate decisions and perform the duties of the job. An effective and efficient manager will continually look for resources to help him grow in the job.

Get acquainted with Theory X and Theory Y. There are numerous theories that have been formulated about management styles. Theory X and Theory Y, developed by Douglas McGregor, are relatively simple theories based on opposing styles of management. Theory X assumes that people are lazy, dislike and shun work, lack ambition, dislike responsibility, and prefer to lead subordinates to the feeding trough. Theory X assumes that the average human being seeks to avoid responsibility, is not ambitious, and seeks security before advancement.

Theory X assumes people are naturally lazy. People work for money, status, and rewards. The main motivating factor for work is a fear of being demoted or fired. People need to be told, shown, and trained in proper methods of work. Workers need supervisors who will watch them closely enough to be able to praise good work and reprimand errors. People have little concern beyond their immediate, material interests. People need specific instructions on what to do and how to do it; larger policy issues are none of their business. People need to be inspired, pushed, or driven.

Theory Y assumes that people have a psychological need to work and want achievement and responsibility. Under Theory

Y, the essential task of management is to arrange organizational conditions and methods of operation so that by directing their efforts toward organizational objectives, people can achieve their own goals. People who agree with Theory Y believe that, for most people, work is as natural as play; that people have the capacity for self-control; that motivation arises from higher-order needs such as self-esteem and achievement; and that people, if properly managed, will be more than willing to take on responsibility. Finally, Theory Y says that people can be creative and team spirited and that few organizations make use of these inherent abilities that their people have.

Theory Y assumes that people are naturally active: they set goals and enjoy striving to reach them. People seek many satisfactions in work: pride in achievement, enjoyment of process, sense of contribution, pleasure in association, and stimulation of new challenges. The main force keeping people productive in their work is a desire to achieve their personal and social goals. People seek to give meaning to their lives by identifying with larger causes. People naturally tire of monotonous routine and enjoy new experiences. People need to be released, encouraged, and assisted.

The effective boss will use both theories interchangeably. The effective manager will recognize that he will supervise some persons who gravitate toward Theory X and some persons who gravitate toward Theory Y. Theory Y is appropriate for recognizing subordinates for a job well done, developing leadership skills in subordinates, and providing opportunities for growth and development. Most leadership and strategic planning are promoted by the Theory Y management style.

The effective boss will use Theory X when it is necessary to confront an employee for performance problems or negligence on the terms and conditions of employment. Theory X may be necessary for disciplinary actions or constructive confrontations. Theory X can be utilized when a manager needs to use hands-on approach with an employee.

Adopt a pragmatic way of thinking. Creativity and innovation are regarded as threats by government employees. Visionaries are not encouraged or regarded as being intelligent. A pragmatic mind will enable a manager to sort through piles of innuendo to find solutions for common problems. Be practical. You will not be a threat to senior staff or to subordinates. Do not view the glass as half full or half empty. It's simply a glass that has some water in it. Pessimism will earn you a negative reputation, and others will stay far away. Optimism will alienate other managers who do not appreciate the cheerleader approach to management.

Know thyself. A manager must know his individual strengths and weaknesses. Your coworkers will learn your strengths and weaknesses. It's best to be prepared. Embrace both the good and bad of your management style. Surround yourself with coworkers who have the opposite talents and skills. For instance, if you are a big picture–type manager who hates details, find someone who works with details and embrace that individual. No one individual will ever have all the answers. All must work as a team to accomplish the goals of the agency.

Know your people. Know the people you supervise inside and out. Know what they like to eat, where they like to play, and the names of their children and grandchildren. The rewards for knowing as much as possible will pay tremendous dividends in the long-term.

Know your fellow managers. You will have many opportunities to interact with other managers. Many of the decisions made in state government are made among managers. It pays to learn how to interact with everyone for maximum value. Most managers in state government can be divided into six distinct personality types. Each personality has its positive characteristics, and each personality has its negative characteristics. The smart manager will learn to make the most of each personality.

> **The Employee's Manager:** The employee's manager uses Theory Y most of the time. He thinks workers are professional, dedicated, and ethical. Performance issues are usually identified as training issues. He assumes the right amount of training will correct any performance issue. He has friends and family outside the office. He prefers to work forty hours a week and looks forward to time away from the office. His subordinates are encouraged to be creative and innovative. The employee's manager makes the assumption that employees need some level of support and encouragement; however, they prefer a certain amount of autonomy. He understands that all managerial decisions have an impact on agency stakeholders. He keeps the big picture in mind.

The problem with the employee's manager is his obvious reluctance to identify and correct performance issues. He is so focused on job satisfaction that he ignores performance problems. He may fail to correct behavioral issues or performance issues. Some coworkers take advantage of the employee's manager. He may appear to be too laid back. The employee's manager works best with coworkers who are motivated, have initiative, and require very little supervision.

The Detailed Manager: This manager will focus on details. She becomes absorbed in the language of a proposal, contract, or memorandum. She can spend hours changing the wording of a document. The detailed manager is intimately aware of font sizes, paragraph indentions, and incorrect terminology. This manager will review printed information with a critical eye that is able to zero in on misspelled words and inappropriate language. She moves at a slow pace on policy and procedural changes. She is skilled at identifying potential problems with planned activities. Detailed managers make lengthy presentations. She goes into explicit detail to explain a procedure. Detailed managers are attracted to state government because changes are made very slowly and with great effort. There appears to be an excess of detailed managers in state government.

The problem with a detailed manager is that she becomes so focused on a project that she ignores the fact that the project may be obsolete or unproductive. She has difficulty seeing the big picture. Once she starts a project, no one can dissuade the manager about the relative purpose of the project. The manager will continue to work on the project at the expense of her coworkers and taxpayers. The detailed manager focuses on the process and not the end results.

The Manager in Control: This manager has a desire to be in control at all times. He is king of the workplace. He does not fear senior-level managers or subordinates. He is courageous and takes a stand on all issues within the agency. His opinion is heard in the break rooms and the restrooms. He can logically explain his decision making process. It is advisable to make every effort to understand the logic of this manager. However, you must guard against the wrath of this manager. He will challenge anyone who does not agree with him.

The problem with the manager in control is that he thinks he is correct about everything. It's his way or the highway. It is seldom worthwhile to challenge the manager in control. He may retaliate with anger and vindictiveness. A manager in control looks the part. He is regal, dresses well, and is usually highly educated. He has supreme self confidence. You may win a battle with a manager in control; however, you will lose so much energy and time that it will not be in your best interest to enter into battle.

The Manager on Stage: A manager on stage is outgoing and sociable. She loves to be the center of attention. She craves the limelight and will say or do anything to get some attention. She usually has excellent verbal and written communication skills and is frequently used for presentations to large groups. She is popular with coworkers. The manager on stage is responsible for social occasions and usually hosts after-hours parties in her hotel room.

The problem with the manager on stage is her penchant for being friends with everyone. She may have difficulty in separating from friends when she enters into management. Negative attention is better than no attention. The manager on stage may find herself in embarrassing situations because of her inability to control her mouth and her desire to have friends.

The Obsessed Manager: An obsessed manager is determined and driven. Persistence is the key to victory. His mantra can be found in the famous speech by Winston Churchill: Never give up. Never give up. Never give up. He functions on the premise that government work is cyclical.

What goes around comes around. You will get a second chance and a third chance. Be prepared for the breaks. Be patient and be persistent. The obsessed manager will seize every opportunity to present his ideas and gain support from coworkers.

The problem with the obsessed manager is that he is unable to let anything go. A manager must know which battle to fight. But an obsessed manager will sometimes fight for the sake of fighting. It becomes difficult for him to let go of the past. He enjoys a good fight and is motivated by a challenging event. This stubborn disposition will cause the manager to lose support. He may appear too stubborn and too unlikely to change.

The Self-Serving Manager: Self-serving managers are cunning and conniving. They are loyal to no one. The self-serving manager will do anything to increase her salary, receive a promotion, or obtain any type of perk she can from her supervisor. She will abandon anyone who cannot help her achieve her goals for self-survival. You must be aware of the self-serving manager. A self-serving manager will steal your ideas and make them her own. She will steal your good employees. The self-serving manager will cause you to miss work because of anxiety and nervousness. The one positive benefit of working with this management style is that she will inspire other managers to unite for the best interest of the agency and its stakeholders.

The problem with the self-serving manager is that eventually she will bite the wrong person. Be nimble and quick when in the presence of a self-serving manager. She is loyal to no one other than self. Spend minimal time with this manager. She is your enemy and an enemy of the agency and taxpayer.

Recognize and reward staff for making goals, engaging in professional behavior, or showing up at work day after day. Use the first few moments of your day to acknowledge staff members who have accomplished something meaningful to the agency. Recognize five accomplishments each day.

Recognition can be in the form of verbal praise. It may be an e-mail or a handwritten note, card, or memo for the personnel file. You can send a note to the entire office that expresses your admiration for a job well done. Never allow even the smallest act to go unrecognized. Recognition can start a mudslide of praise and happiness. Coworkers will want to pass the warm fuzzy feeling on to others. They will in turn share their compliments and praise with others. An environment where coworkers recognize one another is a happy and productive environment.

Take time to say goodbye to coworkers who resign or retire. They have made contributions to the agency and to the customers. Your coworker will appreciate your efforts and will remember you as a good manager. He will refer to you in a positive manner and will smile when he thinks of you. He will tell other potential candidates who may fill his position that you are a good manager. Attendance at retirement celebrations can become recruitment sessions.

Other coworkers will recognize that you have taken the time to recognize an accomplishment. They will appreciate your efforts and will be more responsive to you. It will be your golden opportunity to pay a tribute to someone who has served the agency well. Offer to make some remarks about the individual. Express how much he has meant to the agency and to the customers.

Meet the honoree's family and friends who attend the ceremony to pay their tributes. They will be pleased that their loved one had such a good supervisor. They will be impressed that you took the time to attend his day of celebration. They will view your leadership as warm and attentive. They will wish that they could have had such a wonderful supervisor.

Keep in mind that someone is watching you. Pretend that you are on center stage at all times and that your performance is being watched by a large audience. This will force you to be thoughtful and careful about your actions, words, and expressions. People will always be watching you and gauging how you react to various situations. It's best not to relax too much.

Develop courage. Confrontation is necessary in the life of a manager. Learn to confront people and conflict in a positive and professional manner. Develop the courage that will sustain you when you know a decision is not in the best interest of all parties. You will be confronted with decisions or behaviors that are not ethical. Do not ignore your inner feelings. These feelings are based on your experience with the issues at hand. We should trust our instincts because they have been developed over time and throughout our lives.

You may not have been born with courage, but it can be developed over time. You will need to have courage when a subordinate accuses you of inappropriate conduct such as harassment or favoritism. Use your courage to confront the accuser. Be calm and nonjudgmental during the encounter and until the issues are resolved. Show no emotion. Simply confront the offense and the offender. Seek a solution that is in the best interest of all parties.

The accuser usually has an ulterior motive, often to divert your attention from her performance or lack of performance. She may not have acquired the skills to perform the essential functions of her position. A complaint may trigger an investigation. You will want to run and hide in a corner. Never run and hide. Be courageous and stand up for your behavior and beliefs. Keep the real issue in the forefront of your thoughts. A complaint and an investigation may delay your performance management process. Stay the course. Be courageous. Don't change your course of action. The subordinate may win a battle. You will win the war. Keep your focus and remain courageous throughout the ordeal.

Develop the likeability factor. Most people can become likeable. Think of people you like and enjoy being around. Imitate their behavior. Likeable people listen to others more than they talk. Likeable people are helpful and focused on helping others become successful. They put others first. Likeable people are humble. Likeable people are respectful of other people's time and attention. Likeable people are positive. They radiate energy and enthusiasm.

Adopt a pet. A dog or cat will remind you that it's the small things in life that are important. Exercise, fellowship, food, and water are the best things in life. A pet will remind you that a word spoken softly is more likely to produce the desired results. A pet will love you despite your flaws.

God blessed my life with River, my dog, in 2008. My regret is that I did not have him in 2001. He's the one living creature that loves me whether I make the right decision or the wrong one. I smile when I take him to doggie day care or when we go for a walk. I laugh when he gets upset about the sound of the vacuum cleaner. I laugh when he barks and chases squirrels out of the yard. I laugh when he plays with his cats, Brooks and Bridges. I love him more than I ever knew I could love a pet. I know from personal experience that loving a pet can keep a manager healthy, sane, and at peace.

Consult with your higher power. Be at peace with the decisions that are made at work. Speak with the Lord. You will not agree with all the decisions or the course of actions taken by some of the managers or politicians. It is important to keep in mind that nothing remains the same and everything changes. Search for the right answers and look for the solutions that are in the best interest of tax payers, customers, and other agency stakeholders. Pray and wait on the best solution. One of my final acts as a middle manager required consultation with the Lord. I had the privilege of working with a group of managers across the state who shared a strong Christian faith. We were asked to sign a letter that supported some proposed legislation. We met for lunch at a cafeteria in central Georgia. We held hands and prayed for the fear that we held in our hearts. We knew we might face retaliation. We also knew we were doing the right thing for our clients, our staff, and taxpayers. We signed the letter and never looked back.

Prayer is the answer to every question.

ABOUT THE AUTHOR

Dianne G. Davis graduated from the University of Georgia in 1980 and from Valdosta State University in 1986. She has a master's degree in industrial psychology. She is a certified public manager and certified rehabilitation counselor. She was employed with the Georgia state government for 32 years. She was employed in the Department of Human Resources, the Department of Labor and the Department of Human Services. She was a regional director in South Georgia with the Vocational Rehabilitation Program from 1997 to 2013.